THERE ONCE WAS A GIRL...

JOANNIE BOWSHER

JB Ink

Packaged by Wish Publishing

Printed in the United States of America
10 9 8 7 6 5 4 3 2 1

Illustrations:

cover background – © Lumikk555/Shutterstock.com

page 5 – © SchottiU/Shutterstock.com

page 7 – family photograph

page 9 – © Kelvin Degree/Shutterstock.com

page 11 – © Fona/Shutterstock.com

page 13 – family photograph

page 15 – family photograph

page 18 – © Victoria Novak/Shutterstock.com

page 21 – © Anastasiya Oleynik/Shutterstock.com

page 23 – © Fona/Shutterstock.com

page 25 – © Denise Fortado/Shutterstock.com

page 27 – family photograph

page 29 – fairies © Lorelyn Medina/Shutterstock.com,

berries © Natalia Alexeeva/Shutterstock.com

page 35 – family photograph

For my family

RATTLE THE GATE

Rattle the gate as you pass by the lane.
Jump in the puddle, ignore the rain.
Sing only the melody, skip the refrain.

Rattle the gate everytime you pass by.
Kick up the dust of the roadway so dry,
then pick up a rock, and just let it fly.

Rattle the gate 'til the katydids don't.
If you wait 'til they do then they won't.
They'll hiss in the way that katydids do.
They can hiss all they want, it won't bother you

Rattle the gate as the ladybugs stare,
and the damsel and dragonflys dart through the air.
A praying mantis down on its knees,
but you shake the gate as if it had fleas.

Rattle the gate as the moo cow comes over.
Not a care in his world, just chewing clover.
He shakes his head and bats his eyes,
swats his tail and scatters the flies.

Rattle the gate though no one can see
but the summer wind and an occasional bee.
And Nana and Papa, who oversee
as I rattle the gate, they let me be me!

DENNY

He gave you the world then took it away
one bright and sunny summer day.
You were the way I wanted to be
beautiful, happy and so carefree.

How sad to leave it all behind
you're frozen there in my mind,
black hair flowing, singin' "little bit of soul."
And then the sadness on the face of Joe.

Thanks for the light you left behind
however short the flame.
Comfort from the great unknown
whenever I think of your name.

MY FIRST POEM

Through these troubled times I trudge,
impatiently waiting on some reaction.
Praying people will not judge what I do,
there's no satisfaction.

The idea that I just exist,
knowing no existing pleasure.
Never seeing what I do
as what my mind holds as treasure.

Could of - should of - would of - too,
they beat me in the ground.
Maybe I just don't want to.
Light stays hidden until it is found.

THERE ONCE WAS A GIRL...

There was once a girl who saw fairies,
of that she thought she could trust.
She was sure it was some kind of magic
that sprinkled the air with a shimmering dust.

There once was a girl who thought a king ruled
with a gentle soul and would always be there.
The King and the Queen would toil unseen,
insuring the girl was never bothered with care.

Her Prince appeared to her early,
brooding and sad but with light.
Everyday she would join in his busy world,
like the tail on a crisp brand new kite.

At times she let down the fairies
with vision too narrow to see
the glow from the glimmering fairies,
for her thoughts were centered only on "me."

So the fairies they dimmed for a while and waited,
and the girl came with a baby in tow.
The fairies knew they could sparkle and flutter their wings,
they put on the grandest of shows.

The girl she so loved the baby,
unafraid, she let the magic run.
And the fairies lit up her doorway,
at the birth of their second son.

The boys welcomed the fairies to play
in their room in the sun.
The King and the Queen and the Prince could be seen
laughing and joining the fun.

There once was a girl who thought she saw fairies.
They danced, and they twinkled and charmed.
As long as she knew she had fairies,
she thought she could never be harmed.

BUT...someone has taken her fairies.
Bring them back – I want to bathe in their shine.
I want to see the glow only fairies can throw
on one whose life was as sheltered as mine.

ROSS

Where are you today my little one?
Who are you today?
What scheme in your internal world
has swept your mind away?

I've been there too,
what a wonderful view.
The best part is it belongs to you,
and they can't take that away.

Those without it will always refuse you the time you need
so that life doesn't bruise you.
I want you to know I respect where you go,
a place all your own so your ideas can flow.
Enjoy your stay.

Say hi to the mans – Super and Spider,
James Bond and all the other crime fighters.
Say hi to them all each and every one.
How lucky they are,
they're with my precious son.

PHILIP

You don't know me or remember
my voice, it escapes your grasp.
But I have been there every September
as we mark another year gone past.

When you smile, my spirit is freer.
My unfinished task a little less.
I wanted you to know me better;
could be that you know me best.

A cartoon gives you simple pleasure.
The laughter pushes out your belly.
Nature is your biggest treasure.
You value time just to be silly.

Don't be afraid and don't feel cheated.
Time extends forever for us all.
I am in your tears when you're defeated.
The air your home runs ride upon.

Look in the faces all around you,
they have the memory of my dying.
But you remember my eyes disappearing,
your memory is of me smiling.

You are the lucky one, Philip.

PHYSICIANS EXCUSE

It started with a ringing deep inside my ear,
numbness in my face, dizziness and fear.
Excessive medication put events in motion,
heart and nerve involvement, roller coaster emotion.
Side effects: accept them as a necessary evil
and a life altering blessing.
And if we can't reverse them,
we'll blame them on depression.

Yes, depression is your problem,
not the lupus deafness-numbness.
Thinking that's your problem
only proves your common dumbness.
Physicians can't be wrong.
It's your fault, learn your lesson.
You see, we don't make mistakes.
It's only your depression.

Now take this sedative, we'll add it to the rest.
Frankly it's for us, you see, you're becoming quite a pest.
Maybe you won't bother us to solve your mystery.
The answers are lost, like your hair,
with chemo hair recession.
Whoops! Wait a minute,
we can't blame that one on depression.

Now be a good girl, go away. You don't fit the mold.
You won't sit quietly, fold your hands,
and do what you are told.

You actually have the audacity to show us some agression.
Of course, that will fade when we medicate.
Poof! No more depression.

Now don't ask me a question that's not my specialty,
it wastes my time. Ask doctor number three
or is it four, or five? Heck, I don't know.
There's so many in my profession.
And anyway, look at you! You look fine.
It must be your depression.

LEMONADE

"Make the best of a bad situation,"
they say as your hair hits the floor.
"Besides when a gal reaches your age,
she doesn't need that long hair anymore."

"It won't hurt a bit," the nurse says,
as she holds your hand through the test.
"Honey, if that's true, take my place.
I really could use the rest."

"Does it hurt when you do that? Don't do that."
How long will it be til you see
any part of your life that hurts, you stop.
By the way, that advice is for free.

Learn to roll with the punches
as your old life starts to fade.
Life handed me a lemon,
and now I'm drowning in lemonade.

LUPUS AS A LION

I know that you control me now, my sleeping lion.
You growl contently as you lay so still.
You will become restless and search and growl for vestige.
You will destroy but hopefully not kill.

Likes waves that wash upon me, I fear your coming presence.
I weep for tomorrow which will rage in me like fire
and hide my pleading cries for you to let me live
while burying the hope to die.

Each day charity from an unknown benefactor,
a gift is given to me —
time to remember so that I can recite the story
and recall the sun in all its glory
before it became enemy mine.

Two tanned and tired faces through the door
into the coolness, toys that were left laying on the floor.
After swimming all the day long,
cool sheets covered with warm blankets
and quiet air around your bodies,
small but strong.

That was truly heaven, summer without a hint of fading.
No school bells ringing, or umpires bellowing "play ball."
Just health, time and my boys together in the sunlight
until the lion came to call.

They say you are a wolf, but I feel you as a lion,
a huge majestic lion sleeping in the moonlight
in the coolness of the evening breeze
and as you sleep, please see me,
me encased in sunlight
as I take comfort in the serenity of my reprieve.

A DYING DREAM

A dying dream came by today,
it beckoned me to come and play.
It looked at me with saddened eyes
and disappointment at my lies.

It's faith in me still twinkled there,
bright, shiny, crystal clear.
I didn't have the heart to say,
"Too late, we can not play."

So I smiled and stretched out my arms,
but my smile could no longer charm.
It backed off and stared and stared.
I could tell that it was scared.

"Where were you?" It spoke so slow.
"I'm weak and fear about to go.
And when I go, a part of you,
I'm sorry, but it goes too."

"Circumstances are all," I plead,
"There were others who were in need.
Their dreams were important too.
I just never got around to you."

"Sentences where I come from
start with 'when' which will never come.
They never start with 'I,' you see,
though I with you would have been 'we.'"

"So I let you down, but be proud of our life.
I've raised a family, been a good wife.
We love each other, and I care for them still.
There isn't a dream of theirs,
I won't help to fulfill."

A dying dream came by today.
It flickered a little but decided to stay.
"If you hang on, I'll hang on too.
Maybe," it said, "you'll get around to you."

AMELIA AT TWO

Amelia sees this, and Amelia sees that.

Fairies that hover with wings so bright.
Fireflies lighting the park up at night.
How the sun on the water makes it twinkle just right.

Amelia hears this, and Amelia hears that.

She shakes and shimmies to each song that plays.
She entertains happily for nothing but "yays!"
Smile and groove, bounce and snap,
and before we are done, she will end with a clap.

Amelia does this, and Amelia does that.

She bobs and she weaves to what she's got going.
Every thought in her mind is a seed she is sowing.
Her purpose is clear with each tiny step.
"I'm planning my entrance, I'm just not there yet."

Napping recharges her for the day.
"I'm awake, Mom and Dad,
where shall we play?
The park? A parade?
What do you want to do?
Let's get going and don't forget Roo!"

Amelia loves this, and Amelia loves that.

Snuggled with Daddy on the couch late at night.
"Disney's OK, Daddy, but Seinfeld's all right."
Mommy cuddled up asleep nearby, they're a team,
"Shush, let her sleep! Our tomorrow is her dream."

EVIE AT THREE

When your world is too ahh and you begin to shiver,
just smile at ahhs —
they'll shake and they'll quiver
from all the joy your smile delivers
Goodbye to ahhs
forevermore.

When your world is too ahh and you're in the dark,
run to the window and look at the park.
Fireflies will light your way
until your sunshine brings a brand new day.
Goodbye to ahhs,
now let's go play.

Ahhs are tiny.
Ahhs are small.
Don't look for them, and you won't see them at all.
Daddy and Mommy, Amelia and Roo will chase them
before you see them too!
Goodbye to ahhs, they're just too eww.

Now your world has no ahhs.
They've taken a hike.
Explore your world.
Do what you like.
This world needs Evies with your courage and grace.
This world needs your spirit and precious face.
Welcome to Evie
all over the place!

THE BERRY FAIRY

Never eat the berries that on the bushes grow.
Always ask your parents first, they'll be sure to know.
Yes, God created berries, but now you will see
why you have to ask someone and how that came to be.

In a land for fairies where cottages lie
made from the teeth that the tooth fairy buys,
lived a family of fairies with two little boys,
right on the corner where Peace Street meets Joy.

Gilyean and Rossi were two fairy brothers.
where you saw the one, you would always see the other.
Gilyean was content to stay in the village he called home.
but Rossi — oh that Rossi! — he had a need to roam.

Fairy dust protected them so they should never stray.
It kept you safe forever, if you never went away.
Fairy dust was in the air and flowed from every stream.
Shimmery gold and silver, God's grace in a sunbeam.

But every chance that he could get, Rossi had to see
the children of the forbidden town
who were as big as they could be.
Climbing to the top of an oak tree hundreds of years old,
Rossi really wasn't good at doing what he was told.

He had heard the stories of the curious ones
who had ventured out of town,
never to return and never to be found.

Though he had been taught these things
and taught them well,
he made a plan to go there, and he was bringing Gil.

His plan was to sneak away at morn
and return before their lunch.
"From the top of the tree it wouldn't be far,"
yet that was just his hunch.
The tree spread out and gave its shade
to the playground down below.
Such fun they would have and no one would ever know!

So they climbed to the top of the old enchanted oak.
Gilyean mustered up his courage, and this is what he spoke,
"Oh Rossi, I am scared, and I am just your little brother."
"Trust me," said Rossi,
"I'll have you home to eat your supper."

Out to the branch that looked out on the kids below,
all the way to the end did the mischievous brothers go.
Rossi and Gilyean sat on the end of a sturdy red oak leaf,
when suddenly up they did go on a sudden strong breeze.

They tried to fly, but without fairy dust,
their wings would not work.
And suddenly with a thud and a quite forceful jerk,
they landed on a bench with berry bushes all about.
"What now, Rossi?" Gilyean cried,
then Rossi heard a rousing shout.

The shouting was from the children,
and it was getting closer.
The shouting was from the children,

and they were drawing nearer.
"Berries, berries!" the children shouted each to another.
The bench began to quake,
and Rossi couldn't find his brother.

The children sat upon the bench
and finished all their berries.
They sprinted back to their playground,
unaware of the fairies.
When Rossi found his brother,
there was nothing he could do.
Without fairy dust to save Gilyean,
there was only one, no longer two.

He carried Gil with all his might back to the enchanted oak.
He scraped some fairy dust from the bark,
and this is what he spoke,
"I can not face my parents or the fairies so dear.
I will wrap Gil in this soft oak leaf,
and I will leave him here."

Rossi sprinkled Gilyean with the dust
and hugged him oh-so-tight.
The rest he sprinked on his own wings
and filled a pouch just right.
To fly away and never, ever to return to his home,
he was now forced to roam and roam and roam.

But his anger grew with every day,
each day that he spent far away
from all he loved and held so dear.
He really was not seeing clear.
"The children did this to my brother.

They had to have the berries, and Gilyean they did smother.
I will poison half the berries, so the children will get sick.
Only half the berries, so they won't know which to pick."

Back in fairyland, at the corner of Peace and Joy,
a wonderful dragonfly returned their littlest boy.
The fairy dust that Rossi had sprinkled kept Gilyean alive
til a parents' prayer helped him to revive.

They sprinkled fairy dust on Gilyean's crumpled wings,
and when he took a breath, they praised the King of Kings.
They dropped to their knees and said a little prayer,
"Please return our Rossi. He is lost somewhere."

So that is why you never eat the berries
that on the bushes grow.
Always ask your parents first,
for they'll be sure to know.

And keep an eye out for the stray brother,
he needs to know his parents love him like no other.
And if you spy Rossi by a bush or under a fern,
tell him that Gilyean and his parents want him to return.

DADDY

To be in the room with you,
your smell ever close.
I know you are my daddy.
How I love you so.

You laugh, I laugh.
You play, I play.
When you're gone just a minute
I will cry while you're away.

You look to me like heaven,
my home from which I came.
When I look up to see you, I see the clouds
and yet we are the same.

You have embraced who I am and
see my mom within.
You would have loved me anyway
no matter who I'd been.

I trust you, love you, need you.
You'll never let me down.
Residing in my heart and soul,
even when you're not around.

In your eyes, you will always see
your baby never grown,
and I will see my daddy,
the best man I've ever know.

ABOUT THE AUTHOR

Joannie Bowsher was born in Vincennes, Indiana where she enjoyed a magical childhood with her parents, her sister and her Grandma and Grandpa Higdon. She loved her home, Gregg Park and Rainbow Beach.

At the age of seven, Joannie moved to Beech Grove, Indiana where she enjoyed living close to her cousins. They especially loved spending time at the Olympia Club.

Joannie met her eventual husband Steve while in the second grade. He was her paperboy at age 13, and soon thereafter, they became inseperable and shared many adventures. They were married in 1978.

The Bowshers are the proud parents of two sons, Ross and Philip. Joannie likes to recall that when they brought Philip home from the hospital, Ross unwrapped his blanket and told his parents that Philip had fingers and toes which seemed to surprise and delight him very much. Philip and his wife Melissa are the proud parents of two whimsical and wonderful daughters, Amelia and Evie.

Bowsher has been battling lupus and other health concerns in recent years, but she faces the twists and turns of life supported by the love of her family.